W9-CFC-456

Consultant Istar Schwager holds a Ph.D. in educational psychology
and a master's degree in early childhood education.
She has been an advisor, consultant, and content designer for numerous parenting,
child development, and early learning programs including the Sesame Street
television show and magazines.
She has been a consultant for several Fortune 500 companies
and has regularly published articles for parents
on a range of topics.

Copyright © 1993 Publications International, Ltd. All rights reserved.
This book may not be reproduced or quoted in whole or in part
by mimeograph or any other printed or electronic means, or for
presentation on radio, television, videotape, or film
without written permission from:

Louis Weber, C.E.O.
Publications International, Ltd.
7373 North Cicero Avenue
Lincolnwood, Illinois 60646

Permission is never granted
for commercial purposes.

Manufactured in the U.S.A.

8 7 6 5 4 3 2 1

ISBN 1-56173-906-5

LOOK LEARN

Sorting

PHOTOGRAPHY
George Siede and Donna Preis

CONSULTANT
Istar Schwager, Ph.D.

HTS ✦ BOOKS
AN IMPRINT OF FOREST HOUSE™
School & Library Edition

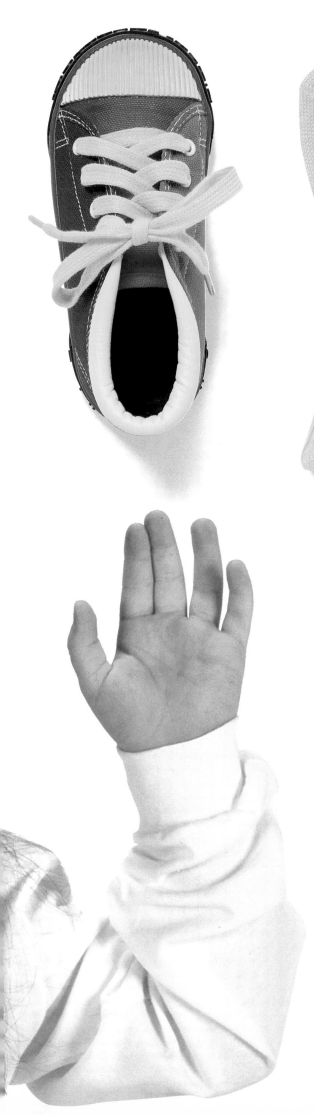

Hold both of your hands
Way up in the air.
What would you put on them?
Can you find a pair?

The big dog likes
    To chase big balls.
The little balls fit
    The little dog's paws.
Which dog wants to play
    With which balls?

This is Rosie.
   She likes red —
Apples, trucks, hats
   For her head.

Point to everything
   that is red.

Sort apples by color;
Help hardworking Fred.
Here's a basket for green
And a basket for red.

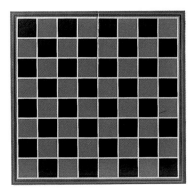

Priscilla the Pirate
Says, "Yo-ho-ho!"
Into which chest should
Each treasure go?

Winter days are very cold.
Summer days are very hot.
Can you sort out all this gear?
Can you tell which boy gets what?

Which things are for summer fun?

Which things are for winter fun?

Let's decorate cupcakes;
　　Add the finishing touch.
Sprinkle some candies—
　　Whoops! Not too much!

What would you never put on a cupcake?

—— Giddy up, cowboy! Get ready to play! ——

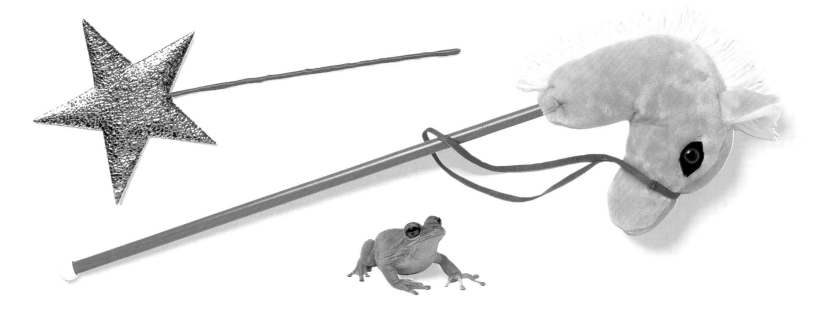

—— What will Brian pick to play cowboys today? ——

When you grow up,
Which things will you use?

Which scissors?
Which tools?
Which glasses?
Which shoes?

For more fun, take another look

Hold Up Your Hands

How many things are above the girl's head?

When would you wear a warm cap like this one?

Have you ever put your shoes on your hands?

Think up a really good name for this girl.

Dogs at Play

Which dog is the puppy?

The big dog's name is Smiley. Can you guess why?

How many balls have stripes on them?

Could the little dog be the big dog's puppy?

Apple Picking

How many green apples are there?

How many red apples can you count?

Have you ever picked apples from a tree?

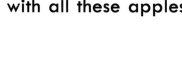

Think of something to do with all these apples.

Pirate Treasure

How many square shapes do you see?

How many star shapes do you see?

What would Priscilla use her shovel for?

Do you think Priscilla is a real pirate?

Baking Cupcakes

Find the things that are not for the tops of cupcakes. What are they really for?

How many candles will be on top of your next birthday cake?

Do you see something that is alive? What is it?

Sheriff Brian

How many hats are in this picture?

Have you ever dressed up like a cowboy or cowgirl?

Who would use the magic wand?

Do you know why cowboys and cowgirls wear hats?

At all the pictures in this book!

Rosy Rosie

What is your favorite color?

Do you see your favorite color here?

Can you think of something red that is not in this picture?

Do you see some things that are alike but are different colors?

Summer and Winter

Count all the things you would wear on your feet.

Have you ever worn flippers?

Can you think of something else you might take to the beach?

How many blue things do you see?

Grown-up Stuff

Do you see some grown-up things that you could use now?

Have you ever tried on a grown-up's shoes?

Do you know how to use scissors safely?

Point to all the kid things. How many are there?